BOb AND RAY

AND
TOM

BOB AND RAY

AND
TOM

*The story of a guy who wrote a lot of
stuff for radio's greatest satirists.*

– by Dan Gillespie –

BearManor Media

Bob and Ray. And Tom.
© 2004 by Dan Gillespie
All rights reserved.

Tom Koch scripts © Tom Koch

All Mad magazine panels © E.C. Publications, Inc.

Published in the USA by

BearManor Media
P. O. Box 71426
Albany, GA 31708

bearmanormedia.com

Typesetting and layout by John Teehan

Cover art by Bobb Lynes

ISBN—1-59393-009-7

Cover art by
Bobb Lynes

Cover: A drawing of Ray Goulding (top) and Bob Elliott (bottom), and a photo of Tom Koch (circa 1964).

With Special Thanks To...

TOM AND DONNA KOCH,
not only for reasons obvious from this book,
but also for their friendship.

E.C. PUBLICATIONS, INC. and THE LEARNING COMPANY, INC.,
for permission to reprint selected portions of
copyrighted material from the pages of *Mad Magazine*,
as presented in the Broderbund CD-ROM set *Totally MAD*.

DAVID POLLOCK,
for sharing his knowledge of and
insights on the comedy of Bob and Ray.

PATRICK LUCANIO, BARBARA WATKINS, and BOBB LYNES
of *SPERDVAC, The Society to Preserve and Encourage
Radio Drama, Variety and Comedy*,
for their help and encouragement in this project,
and for being "keepers of the flame" of old time radio.

CAROL GILLESPIE,
for putting up with my nutty obsessions.

Table of Contents

Intro

I'm a Bob & Ray fan. Or maybe zealot would be a more accurate word. Ever since I first heard Bob Elliott and Ray Goulding on the radio in 1952, when I was about 14, I've thought them to be the world's funniest comedians. I know that most people don't share that extreme view. But a lot of people do, and among them are many of the great comedians that other folks would rank above Bob and Ray.

Although we Bob & Ray fans are avid, I think we were never numerous enough to allow our heroes to become justly rich from their labors. Some B&R fans seek consolation for this in the explanation that one simply has to be a whole lot smarter than average in order to fully appreciate the high humor of Bob & Ray. I don't know whether that's really true, but what's in it for me to argue that it's not?

Ray Goulding passed away in 1990. Bob Elliott is still with us, and in fact turned 80 in May of 2003. To honor that event, RadioArt re-issued its extensive Bob & Ray cassette collection in CD format, and also added a new album, "The Lost Episodes, Volume 5". An announcement of this in the April 2003 issue of *RadioGram* (the news magazine of SPERDVAC, the Society to Preserve and Encourage Radio Drama, Variety and Comedy) drew a slightly testy letter-to-the-editor in the following issue. The letter was from a man named Tom Koch (pronounced Cook), and he said that, as a long-time writer for Bob & Ray, he had written many of RadioArt's "lost episodes," and they haven't been lost at all: They've been stored in cartons in his garage.

What's that? Bob and Ray, masters of comedy improvisation, and purveyors of an almost inimitable form of humor, had a *writer?* Surely not, I thought! A more plausible explanation is that this guy, perhaps under the pressure of approaching senility, had just awakened one morning with the idea stuck crosswise in his brain that he had been Bob and Ray's writer in his younger days. Not a bad way to go though, I mused. And I wondered if I could find a psychiatrist who, by putting me through regression therapy, might implant in my brain some such happy illusion.

A short time later I got to meet Tom Koch, and to talk with him at length. I found him to be immediately likeable, and a very long way from being senile, or "soft as a grape" as Mary McGoon would put it. It quickly became clear to me that Tom did indeed write many of Bob & Ray's sketches, although not all of them. It also became clear that Tom has not received the recognition that is due him for that work.

In an attempt to rectify this, I'd like to introduce Tom to you, and give you some idea of what he wrote for Bob & Ray and how he came to write it. I'll also tell you why I think we can celebrate the work of Tom Koch without having to reduce in the slightest our assessment of the comedic genius of Bob Elliott and Ray Goulding.

In the 52 years that I've been a fan of Bob and Ray, I never got to meet either one of them. But I think that getting to meet Tom Koch is the next best thing.

Here's Tom

Thomas Freeman Koch was born on May 13, 1925, which makes him two years younger than Bob and three years younger than Ray. Although born in Charleston, Illinois, Tom considers himself a Hoosier. When he was only 6 months old his parents moved to Broad Ripple, Indiana, now a part of Indianapolis, and that's where he grew up. After receiving his high school diploma in 1943 he was declared 4F for the WWII draft, so he enrolled in Northwestern University. He graduated from there in 1946 with a B.S. in Journalism, and began what would turn out to be a long career as a writer for radio and television.

Tom initially found employment in Chicago, first as a press service sports writer, then as a news writer for Chicago's CBS radio affiliate, and eventually as a writer for the NBC TV game show *Welcome Travelers*, a show that Tom dryly recalls "would give cancer victims a 9 by 12 rug to solve their problem." He also continued his studies at Northwestern University, and in 1951 he earned an M.A. in Far Eastern Affairs.

When the *Welcome Travelers* show left Chicago in early 1955, Tom left too, for what he hoped would be greener pastures in New York City. He landed a job there on the large staff that NBC was assembling for its ambitious new radio show *Monitor*, the weekend magazine-of-the-air that would last into the mid-1970's. Tom initially hired on as a news writer, but he never got to write any news; instead, he was assigned to do what was called "continuity writing," in which capacity he wrote for several of *Monitor's*

3

hosts. One was Dave Garroway, who was already famous as the host of NBC TV's *Today Show*. Garroway's intimate, low-key style posed a problem for most *Monitor* writers, but Tom found that he could handle it. However, Tom found that he could not handle the stresses of the New York City environment—living on low pay out in Queens with a wife and a young child, and commuting to Manhattan to help put together the hectic 40-hour weekend broadcast marathons. So, after only five months in New York City, Tom took what amounted to an extended leave of absence from *Monitor*, and he moved to St. Louis to live with his in-laws.

It was then, in the Fall of 1955, that the *Monitor* producer in New York for whom Tom had been working suggested that Tom try his hand at writing some "speculation scripts" for the 5-minute *Bob and Ray* segments that had just begun to air on *Monitor*. Having no other work, and no income, Tom agreed. He wrote some sketches and mailed them off to Bob and Ray in New York. "I sent them ten scripts," Tom told me. "They accepted eight, and sent me a check. I kept on sending them scripts, and they kept on sending me checks. It was nearly that simple—we never had a formal contract."

In 1957 Tom took on the additional chore of writing scripts for the 4-minute *Fibber McGee & Molly* segments on *Monitor*. For awhile in 1957-58, Tom was turning out each week 10 B&R scripts, 10 F&M scripts, and 10 scripts for comedian George Gobel, who had also joined the celebrity line-up on *Monitor*.

Tom's work for *Monitor* ended in 1959. But his writing for Bob and Ray would continue for a grand total of 33 years. There were hiatuses, some of which lasted for years: "They would lose a show," said Tom, "and that would be the end of it until they got another one." Tom's association with Bob and Ray spanned, in addition to their *Monitor* segments, their Mutual network radio show in 1955-57, their shows on local New York City radio stations WHN in 1962–65 and WOR in 1973–1976, and finally their three series on NPR in 1983, 1984 and 1987.

In all, Tom wrote 2,980 *Bob & Ray* scripts. Of those, only two, from the very first batch, were ever rejected. As lifetime batting averages go, that's not bad. And as numbers of script pages go, that's a lot.

In 1958, Tom moved from St. Louis to the Los Angeles area. He has lived there ever since, writing (under contract) for such television entertainers as Dinah Shore, Ernie Ford, Jonathan Winters, and Pat Paulsen. "I also wrote for some of the worst TV sitcoms ever to air," he said, "like *My Mother the Car* and *My Living Doll*, as well as a couple of the best: *The Lucille Ball Show*, and *My World And Welcome To It*, which was based on short stories by my boyhood hero James Thurber."

To top all this off, during the period 1957-95 Tom wrote occasional pieces for *Mad Magazine*. Occasional? By one *Mad* fan's meticulous count, Tom's writing has appeared in at least 178 issues of that repository of culture.

Tom remarried in 2000, and he and his wife Donna are now enjoying retirement in a comfortable condominium in Laguna Woods, California, just south of Los Angeles.

Writing for Bob & Ray

Tom typed his B&R scripts on a manual typewriter, using the traditional two-finger method favored by no-nonsense newspaper reporters in black & white movies. (Donna is doing her best to ease Tom into the personal computer age, but he still prefers a manual typewriter.) Bob and Ray needed five copies of each script—two for them, one for the director, one for the sound effects man, and one for the organist. In those days before Xerox, that meant carbon copies. Tom found it most economical to buy 7-copy carbon sheets which were already being manufactured for a Los Angeles television station, and that allowed him to keep two copies for himself. In the upper left corner of each script page Tom put a "slug title" for the sketch; in the upper center he put the script page number; and in the upper right corner he put his name and a sketch serial number. His serial numbering system changed occasionally as the venues for the show changed.

Sadly, the first 1,800 of Tom's 2,980 B&R scripts got destroyed in 1964 by a flood, in a basement where they were being stored. Of the surviving 1,180 scripts, Tom keeps one set at his home and has donated the other set to the Ventura County Public Library in Thousand Oaks, California.

Tom's interaction with Bob & Ray was mostly long distance. "And it was always with Bob, never with Ray," he said, "which was evidently how they chose to divide up their responsibilities. We corresponded mostly by mail, although once in a while we would talk on the phone. Bob typed all his letters to me himself—I don't think they had a secretary."

"I was in their office several times," Tom continued. "It was in a shabby old office building in Manhattan, on Lexington Avenue. I remember it as a suite of several rooms that contained mostly file cabinets—for all their stuff I guess."

Well, I think most of us Bob and Ray fans imagined much grander digs for our heroes. Maybe that's because it was easy to lose sight of the fact that their frequent on-air reference to a vast and highly diversified "Bob & Ray Organization" was just a part of their act. But then, their later books and albums all bore the imposing stamp "© Goulding-Elliott-Greybar Productions, Inc." So weren't we entitled to infer that Bob and Ray had, in a certain Mr. Greybar, a powerful, behind-the-scenes financial backer who would see to all their needs? I learned from Tom that "Greybar" was simply the name of that shabby old office building in Manhattan where they had their offices.

The Books

Three books of Bob & Ray sketch scripts have been published:

- *Write If You Get Work: The Best Of Bob & Ray* (1975, Random House, New York), with a foreword by Kurt Vonnegut, Jr.

- *From Approximately Coast To Coast ... It's The Bob and Ray Show* (1983, Atheneum, New York), with a foreword by Andy Rooney.

- *The New! Improved! Bob & Ray Book* (1985, G.P. Putnam's Sons, New York), with a foreword by Garrison Keillor.

The three famous foreword writers here are all admirers of Bob and Ray, as their words there will attest. Ironically, Kurt Vonnegut, Jr. and Tom Koch attended high school together in Indianapolis, at the highly regarded but now gone Shortridge High School (which counts among its later alumni Senator Richard Lugar and writers Dan Wakefield and Jeremy Larner). Kurt was only a year or two ahead of Tom at Shortridge, but they never became acquainted, then or later.

When the first of these three books came out I bought it, because I could never pass up anything by or about Bob and Ray. But I remember thinking at the time: this isn't going to work – it's got to have their voices. Much to my amazement, though, it did work. The reason, as Andy Rooney explained in his foreword to their second book, was that "if you've ever heard them at all, you can hear every inflection in their voices as you read these words they spoke." Indeed, all three books have that magical quality – you can hear their voices. I had no reservations about buying the two later books.

I asked Tom if he had a similar aural experience when he wrote his B&R sketches. "Yes," he replied. "Anything written for radio or TV requires you to hear the voices of the actors as you write."

I wanted to find out from Tom which of the sketches in these three books he might have written. Now, if you or I had written a particular sketch for Bob & Ray, we wouldn't have any trouble re-calling it, right? But for Tom that's not so easy. After all, he wrote over 2900 B&R sketches, stretching back in time over 45 years. Also, he told me, he tried to discipline himself by allowing no more than one hour to write any one sketch! So they flew by pretty fast.

Tom was able to identify some of his sketches quite easily. But others he could identify only indirectly: by their reference to some small Midwestern town, like Logansport, Indiana; or by their use of last names derived from neighborhood merchants or kids in his 6th grade class; or by their use of names of local sports heroes, like Milt Galatzer and Frank Lautenschlager; or by their use of colloquial-isms that no non-Hoosier would be likely to know. On the other hand, a script that mentioned some small town in New England or upstate New York, like Herkimer, could be chalked up to Bob and Ray, who were both New Englanders. This Sherlockian game of clue-hunting made the task of sifting through all the sketches in the books more fun than Tom had thought it would be.

The result: Of the 146 sketches in these three books, Tom was able to identify 77 as his. A detailed breakdown on individual sketches is given in the Appendix, but in broad summary Tom wrote 46% of the sketches in the 1975 book, 50% of the sketches in the 1983 book, and 64% of the sketches in the 1985 book.

In spite of these remarkable statistics, Tom's name appears only twice in these three books: Once in the first book, at the bottom of the copyright page in an unspecific "grateful acknowledgement", and once in the second book, on a separate dedication page that reads:

To *Tom Koch*, For Help Beyond Measure.

It might seem like a no-brainer here that these books all should have been presented as *jointly* written by Bob and Ray and Tom, but it's not entirely that simple. These books owed their success not only to the cleverness of the writing, but also to the fact that the reader could infuse that writing with the remembered voices of Bob & Ray, "playing" it like a recording. As a rule, bare scripts don't make successful books. The exception in this case occurred mainly, and arguably solely, because of the connection to Bob & Ray's earlier radio performances. So a proper representation would have to be something along the lines, "Sketches written by Bob Elliott, Ray Goulding, and Tom Koch, as originally performed on radio by Bob Elliott and Ray Goulding." But most publishers would probably be uncomfortable with a convoluted handle like that.

The words of dedication in the second book certainly make clear the sincere sense of indebtedness that Bob and Ray felt toward Tom. And Tom told me that Bob and Ray did pay him for the re-use of his material in these books, in addition to what they paid him originally for its use in broadcast. But still, in the final analysis, Tom's role as the writer of roughly half of the sketches in these books should somehow have been made clear to the reader. We'll return to this point later.

The RadioArt Recordings

In 1981, Bob and Ray became associated with Larry Josephson, who later produced their three series on NPR in 1983, 1984, and 1987. Josephson subsequently performed a great service for Bob & Ray fandom, and posterity in general, by collecting and professionally restoring the widely scattered recordings of Bob & Ray performances, many of which had been bootlegged off-the-air by holding a microphone up to a radio speaker. Josephson then made these recordings available for purchase through his company, RadioArt, in the form of 4-hour albums of cassettes or CDs.

At this writing there are a total of 21 B&R albums in the RadioArt collection. Like many Bob & Ray fans, I bought all those cassette albums as they came out, and am now debating whether I can afford to replace them with their pricier CD versions. (Maybe I'll convince myself that I have to do this for the sake of my grandchildren.)

The crediting of Tom Koch in these RadioArt albums is very uneven. The earliest issue was the four-album set "The Best of Bob & Ray," which consists mostly of sketches from the NPR shows. Despite the fact that many if not most of the NPR sketches were written by Tom, he is not credited at all on the first three of those albums. The fourth album comes through nicely with "Written by Bob Elliott, Ray Goulding and Tom Koch." But later albums credit Tom simply with the line "Additional Material by Tom Koch," a tag that seems inadequate in many cases; for example, most of the sketches in the album "Classic Bob & Ray,

Vol. 4" appear to be Tom's. In fairness, it's not easy to identify at this late date who wrote what. Perhaps some future radio historian will undertake the laborious task of doing that accurately.

In any case, these RadioArt recordings are without question the best way to enjoy the comedy of Bob and Ray today. They can all be purchased through the "official" Bob and Ray internet website, **bobandray.com**, which is run by Larry Josephson. This website also serves as the clearinghouse for the recently established *Bob & Ray Permanent Archive*, which is supported in part by grants from The National Endowment for the Arts, and the National Academy of Recording Arts and Sciences (the Grammy® people).

On a more somber note: In a 1996 interview with reporter Michael Ollove of *The Baltimore Sun* (as published in the January 1, 1997 *Los Angeles Times*), Josephson confirmed rumors that Bob and Ray had broken with him in the late 1980's, and that in fact Bob will no longer even speak with him. The break apparently occurred at about the time the B&R RadioArt recordings started coming out. Josephson told Ollove that the Bob & Ray segment of his RadioArt business was not especially lucrative, but of what gross receipts there are, he sends 10% to Bob and the estate of Ray. I regret to report that Tom Koch has received nothing from these sales.

Just Ghosting Along

How did it happen that Tom Koch remained so invisible for so long? Part of the answer to this question is that Tom never had an agent overseeing his working relationship with Bob & Ray. That relationship began very informally, apparently without legal types on either side, and it just stayed that way. Furthermore, it began at a time when most entertainers, especially comedians, did not feel an obligation to introduce their writers to their audiences.

"Fibber McGee & Molly always credited their writers," said Tom, "and Jack Benny was at least open about the fact that he had writers. But practically everyone else kept quiet about them. I think Bob and Ray in particular felt that a great deal of their success depended on the fact that people believed that they made up their stuff as they went along. So they were always careful to hide the fact that they had a writer."

"A friend of mine here in California, a big fan of Bob and Ray, used to live in New York," Tom continued, "and he would often hang around the studios when they were on the air. He told me that he regularly noticed that one corner of their script pages was always notched out, and he never knew why. We figured out that it was the corner with my name on it."

In thinking about this, we should keep in mind that anything that increased the popularity of a radio show benefited everyone connected with it, including its writers. Down in the trenches the radio entertainment business was an iffy way to make a living, and for most people just staying employed and turning out the next

15

show were the main goals—not keeping a who-did-what scorecard for the benefit of future historians. Maybe Bob and Ray reasoned that, if fostering the notion that they improvised not just some but all of their sketches got them a bigger listening audience, then surely everyone connected with the show would want to do that. Nothing personal. Just show business.

Today such tactics are pretty much a thing of the past, thanks to the Writers Guild. Also, audiences have come to recognize that great performances are a joint product of talented performers and talented writers, and those talents need not come packaged together. But if you've already started down the old path, it's not so easy to make the jump to the new one.

When Ray died in 1990, after a long bout with kidney disease which had for all practical purposes ended their act two years earlier, Tom sent Bob a letter of sympathy, along with a clipping of Ray's obituary from the *Los Angeles Times*. Bob replied in a letter which he evidently typed himself, on a manual typewriter, at his home in Manhattan. Bob's letter is both poignant and revealing:

March 29, 1990

Dear Tom,

Thanks for your letter re Ray, and the LA Times obit, the first copy of several I'll probably be receiving from friends out there. I had a little feeling of guilt that the notice included credit for many skits of your design – but that's how history gets changed.

As a matter of fact, Liz *[Ray's wife]* told me at Ray's wake a few nights ago that during his last hours (when he was miraculously quite lucid) he expressed regret at our taking credit years ago for the bits in Mad Magazine. I reminded her that (if my own memory is correct) those were picturizations of pieces you had written for Monitor, and that the monthly features did actually credit the artist (Mort Drucker, I think) and the writer, Tom Koch.

Anyway, it's finally over, and the sadness can be put away, slowly. But not, of course, the memories. We had such great times for so many years that any rough spots we may have faced have faded into nothing. It was indeed a fortuitous bit of fate that brought us together in the first place, and a lucky star that shown over us both that allowed us to chalk up a 44 year association!

[Bob continues his letter to Tom with some remarks about his present and planned activities, and then concludes]...I hope there will be a project arise that's appropriate for your help! I'd certainly like to think that there may be something on which we could collaborate. And please know how very much Ray and I both have appreciated what you have done for us over the years. I'll keep in touch. Best wishes to Lucille [*Tom's wife in 1990*], and sorry we can't look forward to a visit this summer.

All the best,
[signed] Bob.

The "bits in *Mad Magazine*" that Bob mentioned appeared in 1957-59, during a period when *Mad* was running comic-book style sketches starring famous comedians of the day. There were twelve Bob & Ray sketches in all, and at least six of those were taken from scripts originally written by Tom (we'll discuss them in more detail later). "That's how I got started with *Mad*," said Tom. "They used my scripts, paying me something like $50 apiece, and then adapted them to a comic book format." But contrary to Bob's recollection, none of the *Mad* B&R sketches explicitly credited Tom as the writer. (Back then, though, *Mad* gave explicit credit only to its artists, not its writers; however, *Mad* did give Tom explicit credit for his later non-B&R writings for them.)

The wish expressed by Bob for a future project that he and Tom might collaborate on was never fulfilled. In fact, this letter from Bob in 1990 would be their last communication for over a dozen years.

Consummate Actors

The early years of the Bob & Ray comedy team have been documented in several places, perhaps most extensively in a "Profiles" article by jazz critic Whitney Balliett in the September 24, 1973 issue of *The New Yorker* magazine. Briefly, Bob and Ray first met in 1946, as new hires of Boston radio station WHDH. Bob did a morning record show, and Ray gave the hourly morning news reports. "We found out almost instantly that we were on the same wavelength," said Bob, "and after the news we'd bat back and forth a little." This impromptu banter eventually got them a 25-minute show of their own, airing just before WHDH's broadcasts of the Braves and Red Sox baseball games, called *Matinee with Bob and Ray*—a rhyming that determined the order of their names. In this casual setting, they developed their ad-libbed, off-the-wall, satirical approach to humor. In 1951 they were lured away from Boston to New York City for a daily 15-minute radio show on NBC, and that quickly led to a succession of increasingly popular shows on both radio and television, and over several different networks.

By the time Tom Koch began writing for them in the Fall of 1955, Bob and Ray were already well established in the public consciousness as talented comedians with a unique approach to comedy. I know that I was already hooked on them by then, and many of their characters and routines had become firmly etched in my mind: ace reporter Wally Ballou, especially his interview with the cranberry grower; Mary McGoon, B&R's "everywoman"; sportscasters Biff Burns and Steve Bosco; the soap operas like *One Fella's*

Family, and *Aunt Penny's Sunlit Kitchen*, and their epic *Mary Backstayge, Noble Wife*; the adventure shows like *Jack Headstrong, All-American American*, and *Lawrence Fectenberger, Interstellar Officer Candidate*, and *Matt Neffer, Boy Spot Welder*; mystery shows like *Mr. Trace, Keener Than Most Persons*; regular studio guests like Webley Webster, Barry Campbell, Word Carr, Kent Lyle Birdley, and Charles the Poet; the Bob & Ray Overstocked Surplus Warehouse; the game shows like *Ladies Grab Your Seats*, and Arthur Sturdley's *No Talent Hunt*, and Ralph Smedley's *This Is Your Bed, You Made It Now Lie In It*; and of course their many "commercials" and impromptu interviews with "visitors" in their studio audience.

So far as I know, practically all of this material was created, indeed improvised, by Bob and Ray themselves. In the Balliett interview, though, Bob said that he and Ray had gotten some writing help shortly after they came to New York in 1951, this from an early radio comedian named Ray Knight. "He was a funny man and an early influence on me," said Bob, "and eventually he became a close friend." Ray Knight died in February of 1953, at the age of 54, and Bob Elliott later married his widow, Lee. I asked Tom if he knew whether anyone else had ever written for Bob & Ray. "It's rumored that in the early days Andy Rooney wrote a few things for them," replied Tom, "and I know for sure that a guy I worked with in television named Tony Webster wrote a few things for them. But I think that was about it."

Sometime later, I had a chance to talk with David Pollock, a TV comedy writer whose list of credits include *Steve Allen, Mary Tyler Moore, Frasier*, and *M*A*S*H*. As a professional and personal friend of Tom Koch (although 14 years his junior), and himself a huge fan of Bob & Ray since the early 1950s, Pollock has developed an extensive knowledge of the history of the comedy duo. He confirmed that Ray Knight did indeed make a significant contribution to their early repertoire, perhaps being "to a large extent responsible for defining the distinct Bob & Ray sensibility." Typical of Knight's work is the "Chocolate Wobblies" offer by the Bob & Ray Overstocked Surplus Warehouse, which was made after "one of our alert uniformed attendants" stored a large shipment of chocolate Easter rabbits too close to the steampipes. Each Chocolate Wobblie was guaranteed to contain, somewhere inside it, a real purple ribbon. And Knight's earlier work in advertising at Young and Rubicam was no doubt responsible for such fondly remembered Bob & Ray commercials as the one for "Grit— the paste that makes your hands look dirty for that honest, working man's appearance," enabling you to avoid looking like you "live on inherited wealth."

Regarding Andy Rooney, Pollock said that he once asked Rooney if he had ever written for Bob and Ray. Rooney replied that his past comedy writing clients included Gary Moore, Victor Borge, Arthur Godfrey, and Sam Levinson; however, he didn't explicitly put Bob and Ray on that list. As to other writers, Pollock learned (partly from Bob Elliott himself in the early 1990s) that there were indeed some who preceded Tom Koch. On the one-hour Saturday night *Inside Bob & Ray* show in 1951, Art Henley was a credited writer. Tony Webster came aboard in early 1952, but left later that year to write for Sid Caesar's *Your Show of Shows*. Then came Billy Friedberg, who some years later would work for *The Phil Silvers Show*. And following Knight's death in early 1953, Jack Roche, who had earlier worked on *Duffy's Tavern*, contributed material. "However," said Pollock admiringly, "nobody ever wrote nearly as much for Bob and Ray, or for nearly as long a time, as Tom did."

Much has been made of Bob and Ray's talent as writers and improvisers, and I think deservedly. But I go along with those who hold that their greatest talent was as *actors*. At that they were so good that we often forgot they were acting. In each show they would play literally dozens of different characters, infusing each with a distinct and totally convincing personality, and switching between them with amazing speed. Their characters never tried to be funny; they all behaved seriously, and often logically, but always in the face of some ludicrous premise.

That ludicrous premise posed an additional challenge for Bob and Ray: They had to persuade their audience to *buy* it. For only then could they parlay what would otherwise be seen as a silly implausibility into hilarious comedy. That they were able to pull that off with such regularity is just one more testament to their genius as actors. Over their theme song "Mention My Name In Sheboygan," their voices drew their listeners into a world where ludicrous premises seemed to be perfectly natural. They eschewed punchline jokes, personal jabs, and off-color references—handicaps that would incapacitate most other comedians. They got their laughs instead by caricaturing the familiar but subtle mannerisms and foibles of all kinds of people, especially radio and television people like themselves, who were mostly just trying to get through the day with their egos intact.

So Bob and Ray were unquestionably on the fast track in the Fall of 1955. But I would hazard the guess that the burden of all the writing and performing they were doing by then was becoming more than they could comfortably handle. If that's so, then the scripts that suddenly came floating in over the transom from Tom Koch must have seemed to them like manna from heaven.

And what tasty manna it was—as you'll see next.

Tom's B&R Sketches

Before listing some of the more significant B&R sketches that Tom Koch wrote, it's appropriate to emphasize again that there are many that he did *not* write. For example, Tom never wrote any episodes for any of the several series mentioned earlier: *One Fella's Family*, *Aunt Penny*, *Mary Backstayge*, *Linda Lovely*, *Jack Headstrong*, *Lawrence Fectenberger*, *Matt Neffer*, and *Mr. Trace*. Nor did Tom write any of the McBeebee Twins routines, or the interview with the Komodo dragon expert, or the interview with the president of the Slow Talkers of America. And Tom did not write one of my own favorite B&R sketches, the cripplingly funny "Two Face West" routine (on the RCA Victor LP *Bob & Ray on a Platter*), in which two rugged cowboys of the Old West wage a valiant but ultimately unsuccessful struggle to get down off their horses.

Tom's writings for Bob and Ray can be grouped into two categories: Material he wrote for already established B&R characters or series; and material he wrote for completely new series with continuing characters of Tom's own creation. "In the later years," said Tom, "Bob asked me to ease off writing Wally Ballou and Biff Burns type interviews, which they thought they could ad lib themselves. He wanted me to concentrate instead on writing parodies of popular shows that required production scripts for music and sound effects."

Of the many sketches that Tom Koch wrote for *already established* B&R themes, here are four that I particularly like:

- The Wally Ballou interview of the man who says he can't tell Wally who he is because his name is completely unpronounceable. He says it's spelled W-w-q-l-c-w. Wally asks his nationality.

    Man: Well, my grandfather came from Iraq originally. And I've got a hunch that when he changed the letters from the Arabic alphabet into English, he goofed something awful."

    Wally: I guess that could be. Do you still have relatives back in the old country?

    Man: Oh yeah, Cousins…and things like that.

    Wally: How do they pronounce the name?

    Man: They pronounce it Abernathy.

    The man goes on to describe for Wally some of the burdensome problems of going through life with an unpronounceable name, and at the end of the interview he wistfully concludes, "I'd like to say hello to my brother on your program, but I don't know how to pronounce his name either."

- The Biff Burns interview with Big Steve Wurbler, whom Biff introduces as the world champion high jumper. Big Steve jumps in to correct Biff: He's the world champion *low* jumper. Biff smoothly suggests that Steve explain the difference to the fans listening in at home.

    Big Steve: You see, in high jumping you stand in a low place and see how far up you can jump. But in low jumping you stand on a high place and see how far down you can jump.

    Biff: I see. Well, of course you and I both know the answer to this next question, Big Steve. But for the benefit of the fans listening in, I wonder if you'd comment on whether that's all there is to it?

    Big Steve: Well, basically, yes. I might just add that if you jump down from a high place and get killed, then the jump doesn't count. That's why my 57 feet 8 inches still stands as an all-time record.

Biff: I hate to come right out and ask what might be an embarrassing question for you, Big Steve. But, isn't this kind of a dumb sport that would only appeal to a big lummox like yourself, who has rocks in his head? *Big Steve:* Well, yeah. I guess you could make a good argument for that point, Biff. But, personally, I think low jumping's got it all over high jumping. I mean, in high jumping, you can strain a muscle or hurt yourself on the way up, or you can break some bones when you fall on the way down. But in low jumping, you only have to worry about what happens to you on the way down.

- The *Mr. I-Know-Where-They-Are* sketch in which Ralph Flinger, "the man who keeps track of the greats and near-greats who've dropped out of the limelight," recalls for Ray a certain society playboy who had been the childhood idol of a woman listener who wrote in:

  Flinger: Oh, for goodness' sakes alive—Wainbridge Van Cortlant. His grandfather made millions selling defective railroad ties back in the nineteenth century, when the Iron Horse was first spanning the country."
  Ray: And tying it together into one great nation, you mean.
  Flinger: Yes—except on the lines where Old Man Van Cortlant had provided the railroad ties. The wood in most of them was infested with termites. So that caused the locomotives to tip over, before they had a chance to tie this country together into one great nation.

- Wally Ballou's interview with Hudley Pierce, president of the Great Lakes Paper Clip Factory in Napoleon, Ohio. This was a part of Bob & Ray's "cross-country search for inflation fighters"—industrialists whose efforts to cut costs and eliminate waste had enhanced the Nation's economic health. When Wally registers his surprise at not seeing any machinery inside the factory buildings, Pierce tells Wally that he doesn't have machinery because his factory workers make the paper clips by hand, from long spools of wire. And how does the factory manage to stay competitive on price when it can turn out only 200 boxes of paper clips a week?

Pierce: We have a very low wage structure. Here, again, we've been able to hold the line on costs. Our average worker makes about fourteen cents a week.

Wally: Well, how in the world could anyone live on that?

Pierce: We don't pry into the personal lives of our employees, Wally. But I understand that most of our people live in caves out at the edge of town. And they forage for food.

Wally: Apropos of that, I noticed that all of the workers were dressed in rags, and seemed to have strips of cloth tied around their feet.

Pierce: Well you can't wear shoes when you make fourteen cents a week. That should be fairly obvious to anybody.

Tom's gift for creating B&R material is perhaps even more apparent in his many sketches that involve entirely new characters and settings. Here are just some of those *Koch originals*:

- *The Gathering Dusk*, a soap opera series consisting of approximately 270 episodes. It dramatized the trials and tribulations of the paranoidal, hypochondriacal, and perpetually confused Edna Bessinger, voiced by Ray's Mary McGoon. "Edna was inspired by my Aunt Ester," said Tom, "who lived in a small town in Illinois, and imagined that everybody was out to get her." In one memorable episode, Edna tells Dr. Harper that her reluctance to get out of bed and go down into the village is her fear of running into David, who disappeared 10 years ago, but whom she suspects has been hiding ever since in the loft of Grimsley's barn. When Dr. Harper reminds her that such an encounter shouldn't matter, since her relationship with David is long over, Edna replies that she must think of the children, Patty and David. When Dr. Harper further explains that Patty and David actually belong to the Ferguson's down the street, Edna professes profound relief at no longer feeling like she's standing in...the Gathering Dusk.

- *Speaking Out*, a regular feature in which listeners would phone in their opinions on controversial issues of the day. For instance, Mrs. Wanda Guber of Roanoke, VA calls in to voice her opinion that her husband "is stepping out with another woman every time he claims he's going bowling."

- *Elmer W. Litzinger, Spy*. An adventure series featuring a secret agent who, in his own words, "works with quiet efficiency on some of the toughest espionage assignments our government can hand out." In one episode, Litzinger introduces himself to a stranger in a Philippine bar by handing him his business card, on which, he carefully points out, his name is spelled out not only in letters but also in the numerical code that is currently being used by the Pacific Fleet.

- The Einbinder Flypaper commercials. "The brand you've gradually grown to trust over the course of three generations."

- *Garish Summit*, a series Tom wrote for the NPR shows. A parody of shows like *Dallas* and *Dynasty*, it weaves "its endless story of intrigue among the socially prominent. There, in stately splendor far removed from the squalid village below, the beautiful people fight their petty battles over power and money." The stories featured the strong-willed and fabulously wealthy widow Agatha Murchfield, her weak-willed son Rodney, and a shady stranger, who claims to be Agatha's long-lost older son Caldwell, whom she can't quite recall having—"there were so many things going on at the country club back then".

- *Squad Car 119*, a long-running series that parodied *Dragnet*. It would open, "My name's Sam Finch. Me and my partner, Ralph R. Kruger, Jr., are the unsung heroes of the police force." Sam and Ralph engage in the realistic, low-key, and hence boring kind of dialogue that was the hallmark of *Dragnet*. But they rarely make it to the crime scene. The episodes usually ended with their car radio crackling something like, "Car 119, disregard that call to meet Unit 71 to help apprehend a suspect. That suspect has now been apprehended, booked and brought to trial. In one moment, the results of that trial." Tom wrote some of these episodes before he moved to Los Angeles, and a friend once pointed out to him that he occasionally referred to intersections between two L.A. streets that ran parallel to each other.

- *Wing Po*, "the true-to-life story of a Chinese philosopher who wanders across the American frontier in search of work." A take-off on the television series *Kung Fu*, Tom says these episodes were hard to write because he had to keep coming up with new Oriental-sounding philosophical profundities for Wing Po to utter. Such as, "I have traveled far in the hope that I may see from below the same tree limbs which the soaring hawk can only see from above." To which the unimpressed saloon keeper replies, "Uh-huh. Do you want to give me your drink order now, or do you think maybe you've already had too much?"

- *The Hobby Hut*, hosted by Neil Clummer, Editor of *Wasting Time Magazine*. Neil would chat with guests about their hobbies. Such as guest Parnell Garr, who does a show-and-tell with his prized collection of oddly shaped fruit and vegetables.

- The Monongahela Metal Foundry commercials. Makers of ingots for the modern homemaker that are "brighter and shinier than old-fashion brands."

- *Hard Luck Stories*. In these, Tom took his revenge on the TV show *Welcome Travelers* that he had worked for in Chicago back in the early 1950's: unhelpful gifts for guests who need help.

- *Mr. Science*, "idol of the nation's youngsters," a parody of the TV show *Mr. Wizard*. Eager, wide-eyed Jimmy Schwab is introduced by Mr. Science to such new and fascinating scientific phenomena as boiling water. Usually, toward the end of the episode, either Jimmy or Mr. Science would carry the experimental quest for knowledge a little too far, with explosive results, and the episode would end with the announcement "Today's broadcast was the last in our current series."

- *Anxiety*, a series that parodied the classic radio show *Suspense*. Each episode is narrated by the famous lecturer and world traveler Commander Neville Putney, who "reaches into his amazing file and brings forth another tale well designed to keep you in...*Anxiety* (with orchestral sting)." Invariably, after the Commander ends his amazing tale, the Announcer anxiously presses him for more details, only to discover that the tale was not nearly as amazing as the Commander had led us to believe.

- *Fern Ock Veek, Sickly Whale Oil Processor*, "the heartwarming stories of a typical Eskimo coed from UCLA." Fern's surname is a phonetic rendering of the last name of an attractive girl in Tom's high school class, who once turned down his request for a date.

- *Bob & Ray Was There*. A parody of Walter Cronkite's show *You Are There*, in which historical events were re-created as if they were being covered by media news reporters. A typical show began, "And now, through the courtesy of the Ashenfelter Whip Socket Company, we take you back to [echo chamber] April ninth, 1872—Harlan Spivey, Jr. invents the safety pin. Bob and Ray Was There!"

- *Dining Out With Bob and Ray*, a series of programs in which Bob and Ray alert their listeners to "some of the lesser known but truly outstanding restaurants around the world." Such as, for example, the Far Rockaway House of Clam Chowder and Soda Crackers, located in Yonkers (the owner's ancestors came from Far Rockaway), where "the soda crackers are flown in fresh daily from Cedar Rapids, Iowa." And the Hoosier House of Gravy in Gary,

Indiana, where diners are welcome to bring in their own mashed potatoes. And the Psychiatrist's Grille, where all the waiters are unemployed psychiatrists.

- *Tippy the Wonder Dog*, "brought to you by Mushies, the great new cereal that gets soggy even without milk or cream." A parody of the TV show *Lassie*, this show told the adventures of bright-eyed young Jasper Witherspoon, his cantankerous Grandpa, and of course Tippy, whom Jasper thinks is "the brilliantist, smartest dog in the whole wide world," although Grandpa has a decidedly different opinion.

- *Lupis Bartlow, Counselor-At-Law.* "Brought to you by the Intermountain Baby Food Cartel, the world's largest packager of mooshed-up vegetables for your little one." A parody of the *Perry Mason* series, one episode has Lawyer Bartlow, with the help of his investigative assistant Tod Berklow, defending in court demure Agatha Benchlow by dramatically calling as his first witness Mrs. Pamela Buntlow...You'd better grab a pencil and some paper for this one.

- *Search For Togetherness.* A parody of the TV soap opera *Search For Tomorrow.* It was usually filled with emotionally charged dialogue in which the characters seemed to forget what was said over 45 seconds ago, thereby allowing the dialogue to be recycled and the story to proceed at the glacial pace that typified soap operas.

- *Rorshack*, a parody of the TV series *Kojak.* "The gripping story of a big-city cop who wages a tireless struggle to find crime wherever he looks for it." Take, for instance, the theft from a liquor store of a cheap bottle of wine—"Chateau Schenectady 1973, which wasn't a very good year, even for Schenectady." The young patrolman thinks it's too minor to bother with, but Lieutenant Rorshack pulls out all the stops.

- *Down the Byways, With Farley Girard*, a parody of *On the Road With Charles Kuralt.* From behind the wheel of his "deluxe motor home," Farley uncovers and shares with us bits of vanishing America. Such as the old one-room rural school-house in Flaxton, North Dakota, where for the past half century Emmett Horvath has been the only teacher for all the local children. With no money for frills such as textbooks, Emmett relies on what he can remember from his own schooling for teaching material. It turns out that Emmett's memory is replete with glaring factual errors. He gets no complaints from the kids' parents, though, since he taught them too.

- *General Pharmacy*, "the dramatic story of handsome young druggist Ross Flecknoy, and his struggle to save humanity at the prescription counter of a pharmacy still technically owned by his aging father." Dramatic episodes with ending teasers like, "Be sure to join us tomorrow when we'll hear lovely Brenda Ashford say…'But I don't understand. I thought all aspirin was alike.'"

- *Stretching Your Dollars*, with Holden Merkley, "the noted economist and comparison shopper." An example of his useful advice to listeners: "The safest things to invest in right now are a straight flush or four-or-a-kind. Either of those investments should yield about a 400% profit in ten minutes, which is quite a bit more than most banks pay."

- *Emergency Ward*. A forerunner to *ER*, telling the adventures of Dr. Gerhard Snutton, "handsome young physician who has not yet established a practice of his own."

- *You and Your Income Tax*, with advice from Mr. Claude Flabbert, former assistant cashier at the Merchants, Planters and Seaman's State Bank of Hibbing, Minnesota. Claude tells us that he also uses the last name Elliott, so that he can realize a tax break by filing a joint return with himself.

- *The Question Man*. A veritable fountain of facts, Wilmont Shriber always has the answer, although it's rarely to the question asked.

- *The Do-It-Yourselfer.* Host Fred Falvy gets you started on such money-saving yet entertaining projects as repairing burnt out light bulbs.

- *Widen Your Horizons.* Guest lecturers, such as Mr. Jason Holgate of the Kalamazoo Tableware Company, teach you valuable new skills, such as how to use a knife and fork.

- *Blimmix,* a parody of the TV series *Mannix.* In one episode, private eye Joe Blimmix gets pummeled by an otherwise friendly man from Rent-A-Thug, Inc., which caters to crime syndicate bosses who are concerned about the rising costs of health insurance and pension plans for full-time hoods.

- *The Financial Advisor.* Dr. Rex Latchford answers letters from listeners asking for advice on how to invest their life savings. Dr. Latchford's principle business is selling rubber trinkets to hang from rear view mirrors, but he's also a notary public, which is what led him into the field of investment counseling.

Well, there are more of Tom's titles that I could list here, but I'm going to stop because I'm sure you've got other things you need to attend to. Let's wrap up this tour of Tom's B&R work with a look at how some of his scripts got used by *Mad Magazine.*

The *MAD* Bits

In the late 1950's, *Mad Magazine* experimented for awhile with cartooned features of famous comedians of the day, such as Sid Caesar and Ernie Kovaks. *Mad*'s Bob and Ray features consisted of twelve sketches in as many issues, specifically issues 34-44 and 47. These spanned the time frame August 1957 to June 1959 (*Mad* did not always come out every month back then).

Most of *Mad*'s B&R sketches were 3 pages long, although a couple were just 2 pages. The artist on all of them was the phenomenal Mort Drucker, who years later would do the cover art for Bob and Ray's first book. At least six of these twelve sketches were written by Tom Koch, specifically the ones in issues 34, 37, 38, 41, 42, and 43. Although Drucker was by-lined for his work in these sketches, Tom was not. This is partly explained by the fact that, while *Mad* always by-lined their artists, they didn't start by-lining their writers until several months after these B&R sketches had appeared.

The fact that fully half of the *Mad* B&R sketches were scripted by Tom, who by then had been writing for Bob and Ray for only about two years, shows how quickly and thoroughly his work became incorporated into Bob and Ray's repertoire. Just a few weeks before their first *Mad* issue hit the newsstands, Bob and Ray were give the Peabody Award for "Best Radio Entertainment—1956."

The following pages show two panels from each of Tom's six *Mad* sketches, along with a brief commentary.

33

(Facing.) **Two panels from Bob & Ray's "Mr. Science" in *MAD* #34, Aug 1957.**
Text by Tom Koch, art by Mort Drucker.
© 1999 by E.C. Publications, Inc.

This was the first of the twelve Bob & Ray sketches to appear in *MAD*. In their introduction to this lead-off piece, the editors of *MAD*, who rarely spent time passing out serious compliments, were almost reverential: "We at MAD have been listening faithfully to Bob and Ray for years, mainly so we could swipe their material. But now the jig is up. Here then, for pay, under their own by-line, we present Bob and Ray's own version of 'Mr. Science'." High praise indeed from those masters of satirical humor. But this intro by *MAD*'s editors certainly left the strong impression that Bob and Ray themselves had written this sketch, a miscue that seems to have troubled Ray's thoughts during his final hours.

(Facing.) **Two panels from Bob & Ray's "Ambiguous Signs, Inc." in** *MAD* **#37, Jan 1958.**
Text by Tom Koch, art by Mort Drucker.
© 1999 by E.C. Publications, Inc.

This is a Wally Ballou interview with Mr. Oscar Ruprecht, president of the Ambiguous Sign Company in Racine, Wisconsin. The premise of the piece is described in the top panel. A variation on this sketch, which Tom says he did *not* write, appeared 25 years later in Bob and Ray's 1983 book. That sketch, entitled "Ambiguous Signs," had Bob interviewing a Mr. Edgar Fanshaw, who designed traffic signs "that are so difficult to understand that they are easily violated." Fanshaw marketed his signs to towns and communities who could derive extra revenue from the resulting fines. Although the later sketch used different ambiguous signs, it ended with a sequence of signs that was clearly inspired by Mort Drucker's side sketch in the lower part of the first panel here, which was *not* in Tom's script!

(Facing.) **Two panels from Bob & Ray's "The National Bannister Sliding Contests" in** *MAD* **#38, Mar 1958.**
Text by Tom Koch, art by Mort Drucker.
© 1999 by E.C. Publications, Inc.

Some of Tom's funniest sketches drew from his earlier career as a sports writer. In this spoof of competitive downhill skiing, Wally Ballou is interviewing Speed Harley of West Allis, Wisconsin, at the National Bannister Sliding Contests. The contests were being held in the spacious lobby of the Jasper County Elk's Club in Newton, Illinois. (Such recondite Midwestern locations are typical of Tom's work, and they often aid him in identifying which B&R sketches were written by him.) Each contestant makes three slides down the lobby's long banister, and their times are then averaged out. Harley tells Wally that, whereas in exhibition or "fancy" sliding the slider goes down face forward, competitive sliders always go down backwards, hunched over to reduce wind resistance.

(Facing.) **Two panels from Bob & Ray's "The Count-Down Man" in *MAD* #41, Sep 1958.**
Text by Tom Koch, art by Mort Drucker.
© 1999 by E.C. Publications, Inc.

This is another Wally Ballou interview – as were nine of the twelve sketches in *Mad*. In this one, Wally is at America's Satellite and Missile Test Center at Cape Carnival, Florida. He's talking with one of the key men there, Dr. Adolph Von Schmultz, the Center's official count-down man. Throughout the interview, Von Schmultz is constantly veering off into meaningless count-downs. And the irrepressible Mort Drucker is constantly augmenting the written script with pictorial adventures of his own devising; e.g., in the lower panel, that's evidently Dave Garroway smiling over Wally's head.

(Facing.) **Two panels from Bob & Ray's "Baseball Report" in**
***MAD* #42, Nov 1958.**
Text by Tom Koch, art by Mort Drucker.
© 1999 by E.C. Publications, Inc.

Here we find Wally Ballou in the clubhouse of the San Francisco
Giants at Seals Stadium, filling time "while we're waiting for the fog
to lift." Wally is interviewing Duane Grubble, a man who, although
employed by the Giants and decked out in a Giants uniform, is not
really a player. As the team's official heckler, he prefers personal
insults, like "Yer sister raises rutabagas, yuh bum!", because he doesn't
really understand the rules of baseball. Curiously, the editors at
Mad consistently spelled Wally's last name "Ballew," even though
Bob and Ray (and Tom) always spelled it "Ballou."

(Facing.) **Two panels from Bob & Ray's "Music Report" in**
MAD #43, Dec 1958.
Text by Tom Koch, art by Mort Drucker.
© 1999 by E.C. Publications, Inc.

Here we find Wally Ballou in Tin Pan Alley, interviewing Filbert
Hoffenberger, who is a "song tester." Filbert tests the lyrics of
songs for big recording companies to find out if they are really
true. The sketch concludes with Filbert testing the lyric "It's a
treat to beat your feet on the Mississippi mud." He concludes that
it's true, and very delightfully so at that. Drucker populates his
Tin Pan Alley street scenes in this sketch with an array of popular
entertainers of the day: Frank Sinatra, Bing Crosby, Rosemary
Clooney, Mitch Miller, Steve Allen, Ed Sullivan, and (in the first
panel) Pat Boone.

Of the other six B&R sketches that appeared in *Mad*, Tom is certain that he did not write four, but he could not decide for sure about the remaining two. Details are given in the Appendix. The easiest way to read these twelve *Mad* sketches today, short of buying the original issues on eBay, is through the Broderbund 7-CD set *Totally MAD* (The Learning Company, Inc., 1999); they're all on CD#1.

As mentioned earlier, Tom's writing in these B&R sketches for *Mad* marked the beginning of a long association between him and the magazine. According to the webpage of *Mad* fan Mike Slaubaugh, Tom's work has appeared in 178 separate issues of *Mad*, and as late as issue 335 of May 1995. Moreover, of the over 500 people whose writing or art has graced the pages of *Mad*, only 14 have had their work appear in more issues than Tom. There is, however, some murkiness in the statistics from the early issues: Tom Koch is actually listed as one of several "Contributing Writers" on the first page of each of the nine *Mad* issues 38-46. Exactly what he is supposed to have written in those issues is not made clear though, and even Tom can't tell at this late date. Since *Mad*'s editorial office was run rather haphazardly back then, these non-specific credits to Tom may not be entirely accurate. It's interesting to speculate, though, on whether they might somehow account for Bob's recollection that Tom had been properly credited for his B&R bits in *Mad*. We'll probably never know for sure. In any case, more information on Tom's long association with *Mad* can be found in selected issues of the *Mad* fan magazine, *The Journal of Madness*.

I examined all the B&R sketches in *Mad* before I got Tom's rulings on them, and there is one sketch that I would have bet money he wrote, but he's sure he didn't. This is the sketch in *Mad* #39, entitled "Big Big Earth." It's a parody of an early TV show called *Wide Wide World*, on which NBC was showing off its ability to get live TV pick-ups from anywhere in the country over their new co-axial cable. *Wide Wide World*'s host was Dave Garroway, who appears in this sketch as Dave Sturdley. The sketch consists of three "live" interviews—the first in Eastport Maine,

the second in Livermore Kansas, and the third in Salem Oregon –
all of ordinary people doing ordinary spring house cleaning. But
Dave Sturdley's majestic narration ties these interviews together
in a way well calculated to bring a nostalgic lump to your throat;
for example, "A rug is beaten in Maine, and it becomes clean again,"
and "And so our magic carpet touches down in New York again,
after another sweep across this Big Big Earth of ours." So I figured, who else but Tom Koch, who had actually written this kind
of stuff for Garroway back when he was on the writing staff of
Monitor, could possibly have written such a dead-on parody as
this? Well, I guess maybe Bob Elliott and Ray Goulding, that's
who else! After all, such finely tuned and delicately nuanced parodies of radio and television were their stock-in-trade.

It's difficult to find adequate adjectives to describe Mort
Drucker's artwork in these sketches. Spectacular, amazing, wild,
inventive, all come to mind, but don't quite suffice. In some of the
panels though, Drucker's irrepressible imagination tends to over-
power the typically low key pitch of Bob and Ray's humor. For
example, in the "Big Big Earth" sketch I just mentioned, Drucker's
visual setting for the interview of the Kansas woman vacuuming
her house was in a tornado! That plot element was clearly not a part
of the original script, and although it was funny and certainly quite
appropriate for the pages of *Mad*, it was rather out of synch with the
intended banality of that interview.

As delightful as these *Mad* sketches are, *radio* was clearly the
optimal medium for Bob and Ray. Connoisseurs of old time radio
have long known that the eye of a camera, or even a great artist, is
usually no match for the "eye of the mind" when one has genu-
inely talented writers and performers. Thus, Jack Benny's vault
was never as funny on television as it was on radio. And skits like
Bob's interview of a man in the studio audience who sounded like
he might be a Wall Street banker, but is eventually revealed to be
wearing a full Indian headdress, really go over best in the absence
of explicit pictures.

Daniel Pollock, in his liner notes to the 1973 Genesis Records
LP *Vintage Bob & Ray*, quotes the duo as follows on this point:

Bob: "We've always felt that radio serves our particular needs to perfection in providing a setting where we can play to a listener's imagination."

Ray: "Subconsciously, we seem to develop our situations with a picture in mind—often a ludicrous one."

To which I would simply add that the control of both the content of that ludicrous picture and the timing of its unveiling to the audience is often very important to the humor of Bob and Ray. And that control is usually denied them by the all-seeing eye of a camera—or an artist. Then too, radio of necessity focuses the audience's attention on the *voices* of the performers, and for Bob and Ray that's surely where all the action takes place.

The Bottom Line

So what's the bottom line here?

Tom Koch wrote a lot of material for Bob and Ray, material that on the whole is just as good as the material they created themselves. For this work, Tom deserves to be recognized and thanked by B&R fans everywhere. I hope that, as a result of this book, a little limelight will finally penetrate the Gathering Dusk that Tom seems to have been standing in for the past 48 years.

At the same time, we should recognize that Bob and Ray deserve the credit for inventing and refining the broad template for their unique brand of humor. Furthermore, they as performers were the key to successfully delivering that humor to an audience. For as many of us know, trying to re-tell a B&R sketch yourself is a bit like trying to demonstrate how Frank Sinatra sang a song: you might be able to sing "I've Got You Under My Skin" pretty well, but it won't have the impact of Frank's rendition.

Pursuing that analogy a bit further, no one ever thought any the less of Frank Sinatra's musical genius because he didn't write the words and music that he sang. So I think we should cut Bob Elliott and Ray Goulding a bit of the same slack. Of course, Bob and Ray have a big edge over Frank on that score: not only did they create much if not most of their material, their phenomenal ability to extemporize in front of a live microphone was truly amazing.

But, like the rest of us mortals, Bob and Ray were allotted only a limited number of hours to toil in the fields. So I'm glad, really glad, that Tom Koch was around to expand their songbook.

And as Bob made clear in his letter to Tom just after Ray died, he and Ray were glad too.

I'll now confess that I began my investigation of Tom's connection to Bob and Ray with a real sense of trepidation. During my lifetime, I have seen many prominent people whom I admired ultimately exposed as being much less heroic than I had imagined. And I was frankly in no mood to see Bob and Ray get bumped from my shrinking list of heroes by the revelation that someone else had been responsible for most of their cleverness. But as it turned out, I found in Tom Koch a new name for my list. And in the process of sorting things out, I gained a deeper appreciation for what Bob and Ray really accomplished as comedians, with the result that their heroic status was only confirmed. I guess some days you just get lucky.

That Tom Koch went for so long without recognition is of course regrettable. It should not have happened that way. But it really seems to me that this was due to the customs and pressures of the time, and not to any dark design. The good news is that this failing is now well on the road to redress.

So let's have three cheers—for Bob and Ray and Tom!

For all that you've given us, gentlemen, thank you very much.

Appendix: Some Details

Here are the complete results of Tom's attempt to identify which of the sketches in the three Bob & Ray books, and the twelve Bob & Ray *Mad Magazine* issues, were written by him. Each sketch is identified by its title and page number. A "Y" by the sketch means *yes*, it was written by Tom; an "N" means *no*, it was not written by Tom; and a "?" means that Tom was unable to decide whether or not it was written by him.

Write If You Get Work, The Best of Bob and Ray (1975, Random House, foreword by Kurt Vonnegut, Jr.):

  N – Wally Ballou and the Cranberry Grower, 5
  Y – The Gathering Dusk, 8
  Y – Prodigy Street, 11
  Y – Elmer W. Litzinger, Spy, 14
  ? – Editorial Reply, 18
  N – Chocolate Wobblies, 23
  ? – The Presidential Impersonator, 25
  N – Biff Burns Interviews Stuffy Hodgson, 29
  Y – Wing Po, 32
  N – WADS Recruiting Announcement, 35
  N – Mr. Treat, Chaser of Lost People, 38
  N – Lawrence Fectenberger, Interstellar Officer
       Candidate, 44
  Y – Hard Luck Stories, 48

Y – Rorshack, 171
N – Preston Turnbridge, Lighthouse Keeper, 175

From Approximately Coast to Coast...It's The Bob and Ray Show (1983, Atheneum, foreword by Andy Rooney):

N – The Bob and Ray Final Closeout Sale, 1
N – Wally Ballou Visits the Sturdley House, 4
Y – Garish Summit – Episode #1, 9
Y – Hard Luck Stories, 14
N – Slow Talkers of America, 19
Y – Monongahela Metal Foundry #1, 23
Y – King Zog's Birthday, 25
N – The Army Amateur Hour, 29
N – Ambiguous Signs, 33
Y – General Pharmacy, 39
? – Biff Burns's Sports, 43
N – Mr. District Defender, 47
N – Forbush Dinnerware, 53
Y – Mr. I-Know-Where-They-Are, 56
Y – Einbinder Flypaper #1, 61
Y – Garish Summit – Episode #2, 62
N – Buddy Blodgett at the Polygon Ballroom, 67
Y – Special Report, 72
N – The Komodo Dragon Expert, 75
Y – Editorial, The Leash Law, 78
Y – Tippy, the Wonder Dog, 82
N – Public Service Announcement: Elephant
        Keepers, 86
N – Martin LeSoeur, Raconteur, 89
Y – Monongahela Metal Foundry #2, 94
Y – Bob and Ray Was There: Invention of the
        Safety Pin, 95
Y – The Do-It-Yourselfer, 99
Y – Emergency Ward, 103
N – The P's and Q's Minder, 108

The New! Improved! Bob & Ray Book (1985, G.P. Putnam's Sons, foreword by Garrison Keillor):

About the Author

Daniel T. Gillespie is a Ph.D. physicist. Now semi-retired, he works as a consultant in computational biochemistry with scientists and engineers at the California Institute of Technology, the University of California at Santa Barbara, and the Molecular Sciences Institute. In addition to authoring or co-authoring numerous scientific articles for various international research journals, he has written two books: *A Quantum Mechanics Primer* (now out of print), and *Markov Processes: An Introduction for Physical Scientists* (which at 565 pages is recommended to readers who find the present book too short). His avocational interests tend towards such flora of the middle 20th Century as radio, jazz, movies, and trains. He lives with his wife Carol in Castaic, California, and can be contacted at GillespieDT@mailaps.org.

For more great books
on old time radio, visit

http://www.bearmanormedia.com

Or write for a free catalog:

BearManor Media
P O Box 71426
Albany, GA 31708

CHECK THESE TITLES!

BearManorMedia.com

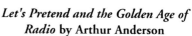

PO Box 71426 • Albany, GA 31708

Spike Jones Off the Record: The Man Who Murdered Music
by Jordan R. Young

20th anniversary edition, newly revised & updated!

$29.95   ISBN 1-59393-012-7

Let's Pretend and the Golden Age of Radio by Arthur Anderson

Revised and expanded, now including a complete log of the show by radio historians Martin Grams, Jr. and Derek Teague!

$19.95   ISBN 1-59393-019-4

It's That Time Again Vol. 2 – More New Stories of Old-Time Radio.
Edited by Jim Harmon

New adventures of Red Ryder, Baby Snooks, House of Mystery, The Whistler, Jack Benny and more!

$15.00   ISBN 1-59393-006-2

The Bickersons: A Biography of Radio's Wittiest Program by Ben Ohmart

Lavishly illustrated, with a foreword by Blanche herself, Frances Langford. A complete history of the program. Biographies of the cast. Scripts. The infamous *Honeymooners*/Jackie Gleason court case. Unused material. And much more!

$19.95   ISBN 1-59393-008-9

Private Eyelashes: Radio's Lady Detectives by Jack French

Phyl Coe Mysteries, The Affairs of Ann Scotland, Defense Attorney, The Adventures of the Thin Man, Front Page Farrell...radio was just full of babes that knew how to handle themselves. Get the lowdown on every honey who helped grind a heel into crime.

$18.95   ISBN: 0-9714570-8-5

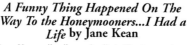

A Funny Thing Happened On The Way To the Honeymooners...I Had a Life by Jane Kean

Jane Kean tells all—and tells it like it was. Jane Kean, star of Broadway, films and television, has had a career that has spanned 60 years. Jane is perhaps best known as Trixie in the award-winning television series, *The Honeymooners*.

$17.95   ISBN 0-9714570-9-3

**For all books and more, visit www.bearmanormedia.com
or write books@benohmart.com. Visa and Mastercard accepted.**

Printed in the United States
153039LV00005B/157/P

9 781593 930097